iPHONE 12

USER GUIDE

**A Simple Guide To Unlock
Hidden Features, With
Screen Shot Tricks And
Tips Of The New iPhone 12
For Amatures And Seniors.**

By

Damian J. Young

Table of Contents

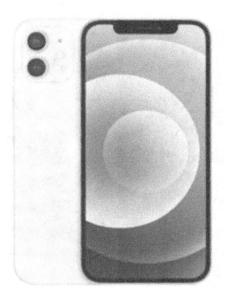

CHAPTER ONE

NEW IPHONE 12: THE REVIEW

The iPhone 12 was finally in power, unveiled with the iPhone 12 Mini, iPhone 12 Pro, and iPhone 12 Pro Max during the company's launch in October.

So what can we learn about the new iPhone? We do almost everything before the iPhone 12 release date, it is scheduled for October 23rd.

The company has confirmed that by 2020 all iPhone products will be ready for 5G, so it will take you to your phone with the speed of browsing.

The four handsets feature, including new colors, a lot of rear camera adjustments, the internal power of each phone, and other features.

Below we will cover every price we learned about the new iPhone 12, including the prices unveiled by Apple Play, the date of delivery, details, and new features.

Want to know more about top-end phones? Here is the iPhone 12 Pro

It is also a small phone, called the iPhone 12 Mini

Each phone will be compared: iPhone 12 vs iPhone 12 Mini vs 12 Pro vs 12 Pro Max

iPhone 12 Key Facts

Orders will now be open from 23 October

Price

What is the price of the iPhone 12? It starts at 799 / $ 799 / AU $ 1,349

iPhone 12 days delivery and free shipping

The release date of the iPhone 12 is set for October 23rd, and you can place an order with Apple from now on.

You cannot pre-order the iPhone 12 Mini until November 6, when the phone will be released on November 13.

Apple Play has confirmed that the iPhone 12 will start at 7 99 in the US, which is 100 dollars more than the iPhone 11 package. This may be due to the introduction of 5G technology.

What is the price of the phone in your market? Below are 12 iPhone prices for the US, UK, and Australia.

In the U.S, you can integrate the device with AT&T, Sprint, T-Mobile, and Verizon. In the UK it can also be purchased from EE, Vodafone, O2, There, and many other networks. We don't know what sponsors in Australia support phones.

iPhone 12 design and display

The new iPhone 12 has a 6.1-inch display size and an excellent feature at the very top of the display.

If you have a phone with a small display and you need an iPhone 12 Mini, you can read information about that phone in our small delivery and pricing documentation.

The iPhone 12 comes in five different colors:

- black
- white
- red
- green
- blue

The iPhone 12 has an aluminum frame on the outside, and it looks a little more rounded on older iPhones - the iPhone 5S looks a lot better than the iPhone 11 and its surrounding corners.

The back of the phone is made of glass, but Apple wanted to show that this phone is tougher than the previous iPhone. It uses a new technology against it called a ceramic shield, which means your screen will remain stationary.

How does this work? Corning, the company that manufactures the shield, claims that it is relatively new and that the nano-sized crystals that are embedded in the glass look like glass, but have more power than clay.

This doesn't mean you should throw your phone away, even if it won't stop your device from hitting or dropping.

The iPhone 12 body is 11% more thinner, 15% small, and 16% light than the previous iPhone 11. It typically weighs 146.7 x 71.5 x 7.4mm and weighs 162 grams.

iPhone 12 is Waterproof IP68 and Dust Resistant.

It has a Super Retina XDR display with a 6.1-inch screen, which doubles the size of pixels like the iPhone

CHAPTER TWO

iPhone 12 SET UP

Turn on and install your new iPhone via an internet connection. You can also customize the iPhone by connecting it to your computer. If you have another iPhone, iPad, iPod Touch, or any Android device, you can transfer your data to your new iPhone.

NOTE: If your iPhone has been delivered by a company or another company, check with the administrator for installation instructions.

Ready for setup

The following resources are available to organize and make available:

Internet connection over a Wi-Fi network (possibly a network name and password) or a mobile data service for the carrier

Your Apple ID and password; If you do not have an Apple ID, you can create one at a time during setup

Your credit or debit card statement, if you want to add a card to Apple Pay when logged in

If you transfer your data to your new device, your old iPhone, or your device's firmware

Your Android device, if you transfer your Android content

Turn on and set up your iPhone

Press and then hold the side button or sleep button for 20 seconds until the button logo appears.

If the iPhone is not ON, you will need to charge the battery. For more information, see the Apple Support in your iPhone, iPad, or iPod Touch is not turned on or frozen.

Do one of the following:

Manually click the layout and follow the screen editing instructions.

If you have another iPhone, iPad, iPod, or iPod Touch iOS 11, iPad OS S13, or later, you can use Quick Start to set up your new device. Combine the two tools and follow the on-screen instructions to easily copy your features, preferences, and iCloud keychain. You can restore the rest of your data and information from your iCloud app to your new device.

Or, if both devices have iOS 12.4, iOS 14, or later, you can transfer your data from your previous device to your new one. Keep your tools in touch with each other

You can also transfer your data using an internet connection between your devices. transfer data from your previous iOS device to your new iPhone, iPad, iPod, or iPod Touch.

If you are blind or visually impaired, tap the side button (on an iPhone with Face ID) to change the screen reader, and voice over, and then tap the home button (on other iPhone models). You can also tap the screen twice with three fingers to zoom.

On iPhone, on Android device

Once you've set up your new iPhone, you can automatically move your data from Android Data.

Move your data manually

Move documents from your Android device to your iPhone, iPad, or iPod Touch.

Android version or later on your device, iPhone, iPad or iPod Touch Check out the support over Android document and download Move to iOS.

On your iPhone, do this:

Follow the reset assistant.

On the Internet and Computer screen, click Move Computer from Android.

On an Android device, do the following:

- Turn on Wi-Fi.
- Open Move to iOS app.
- Follow the on-screen instructions.

CHAPTER THREE

iPhone 12 ACCESSORIES

Apple Play chose to do something different from the previous iPhone 12s from the previous iPhones - but that's not all, so you'll see it smaller than the hardware.

The reason for the iPhone 12's impact is to reduce e-waste, and rightly so - most bikes prefer to buy their headphones instead of using a few items, because for example, if you use earpods, you still use your old pair

But if you don't follow the technical reports, it will be difficult to know what's in the box, what you want to send separately, and what attachments you need. That's why we came up with our iPhone 12 tool guide.

What's in the box:

Below will come your iPhone 12 box. Yes, we do not read the documents with the SIM removal tool here.

It would be very controversial if Apple removed the iPhone from the iPhone box, and we don't know what the company will do. Yes, buying your iPhone 12 will put the phone in the box, even if it is nothing else ...

Lighting with USB-C cable

Lightning - from the moment USB-C cable

Lightning - USB-C cable from Apple

A common thing in your iPhone 12 box is a USB-C cable with electricity. You can insert the power end of this into your iPhone, but please note that USB-C is not a 'typical' USB port on your computer or you may find it in some cases at walls at airports, cafes, or similar places.

Some newer computers and laptops have USB-C ports (including MacBooks), but to charge your phone from the wall, you'll need to take a wall charger with a USB-C port. It simply does not include any electrical connection.

What you want to buy:

The iPhone 12 box should not include the following, but it can be purchased to enhance your iPhone experience.

You may have got one of these so you don't need a new one - but you should check it out first. Most wall mounts come with hardware that has a USB-A port - this is a large, square-sized port - but the iPhone 12 cable connects to USB-C - it has a smaller port and rounded sides.

If you need to buy one of these, the Apple website buys one, but it costs a lot of money, so it might be perfect for finding an Amazon USB-C wall charger.

iPhone 12 earphones

The new iPhone 12 does not come with phone case boxes. If you already have some of your iPhones installed with Lightning, you can use them, but if not is it time to upgrade to wireless headphones?

Apple may cross its fingers when you need to upgrade to its AirPods or AirPods Pro, but there are many more options on the market

Some people may prefer earbuds with phones, but if you have one, it's pretty obvious - wireless options can be expensive, and enjoy the honesty of the built-in audio.

You can buy AirPods with numerous Lightning headphones on Amazon at the Amazon website - don't forget to connect the two drives you purchased to a Lightning port.

What you can buy:

While this is not important for the smartphone experience, it is better to improve the way you use your smartphone.

iPhone 12 wireless charger

Wireless is the future, though smartphones and wireless chargers haven't arrived yet

CHAPTER FOUR

NEW FEATURES WITH
iPhone 12

Key features/improvements

Widget

The widget is designed to make your everyday information more attractive and in-store.

Home screen widget

Place a widget anywhere on the home page for comments by the view. Ideal for browsing your trips, activities, calendar lander events, or news stories.

Widgets of different sizes

Widgets are now small, medium, and large in size so you can choose the right information.

Widget Gallery

Between Apple and all your third party widgets. The store displays a number of integration features and high-quality widgets depending on the user.

Weather widget

You can create up to 10 widgets to make it easy for you to use on the home screen. Insert and distribute one widget in another.

Smart presentation

In the Widget Gallery, you can specify a group of widgets that can be changed by Smart Tools, Smart Stack, to get the right widget at the right time based on factors like time, location. , And functions. For example, you can see the Apple News Widget in the Apple Map in the morning, during the day, and in the afternoon.

Siri Widget

The Siri Think Widget uses a smart tool to show you what you can do on your models, such as ordering coffee or starting a broadcast. Tap the tick to do this without starting the application.

Developer API

Developers can customize their tools using the new API, so they can use updated widgets, including the ability to place them on the home screen and display. In the long run

Library

Apple Library website

The Apple Library has a new section at the bottom of your home page that turns all your apps into one simple, easy-to-move section.

Automatically falls apart

All activities on your iPhone are only listed by categories such as welfare, product, and entertainment. The layout of the components is simple depending on the use of the application.

Supporting words

The Library gives you a list of selected apps to find my time, location, or activities.

Use the scroll bar at the top of the app to quickly find the section you're looking for. If you click on the search section, the statistics will be displayed on the computer system, making it easy to change and find out what's in it.

Hide original screen pages

You can hide pages to move to your home screen by making it easy to access the app library. Library New applications released from the Store will be included in the computer library

It has just been added

You can find the latest additions and subtractions from the store.

Compact UI

Call

When you get a call, the whole screen looks like a ball, so you don't have to interfere with your work. Swipe down to lower the call, or swipe down to access phone calls and click answer

Third-party VoIP phones

Available with an app like developer API, Skype to support incoming calls.

Screen phone

When you get a FaceTime phone, the whole screen looks like it. Swipe down or down the flag to access long sessions on FaceTime.

Siri

Siri has a new integration design that allows you to trust the information on the screen and integrate your next project without interruption. When you start the app, Siri appears at the bottom of the screen. When you call Siri, it will appear at the top of the screen for reading. The products have been updated to provide you with the information you need for a new joint design.

The picture

You can continue watching a video or face-to-face phone while you are using another application. Call your partner and you will have the opportunity to watch or host a television show while viewing your email.

Update the image in the window

You can edit the gallery by clicking on the video clip to expand or share.

Move the image to the windowpane in a corner

Place a video window in one corner of the screen.

CHAPTER FIVE

APP LIBRARY IN iPhone

12

IOS 14 is now available for installation!

iPhone users can use the new widgets on the home screen, Apple can talk in foreign languages moment by moment and talk to everyone about this and the improved messaging service. But the best change to Apple's operating system is the addition of a library that allows you to browse the pages of apps on the iPhone from scratch.

In this article, we will show you how you can achieve this great change, and why you are happy. To see what Apple has read about software upgrades, read the general guide to the latest features of iOS 14

What is the library text on Apple iOS 14?

For now, whenever you install the app on your iPhone, it will start ticking on the home screen or connected devices. This means that if you want to download an app, you have to turn to the pages until you find it. Yes, you can go to another page or put it in a folder, but it will still be on the home screen.

This application library will be converted by creating a special section where your degree marks can be found. If you've used an Android smartphone, you'll know this idea, as it has been on the Google tablet for years.

These two things are different, in Android, computers are stored in old to a new order or in-line order. The Apple Library teams will work together according to their religion and will be on display at WWDDC 2020, including entertainment, community, arts, and future entertainment.

Go to Library on iOS 14

You will find the new Library application page to the right of the last page where the applications are now placed. So if you have the home page and other pages, you will find the application library and on the third page, you will be directed to the left.

Large library screen

Before using the library, it is important to understand what is new in the company you are importing.

Staying in Apple Library doesn't make you want to see other screens on the computer. Then new again

But also to hide them. Click and hold the page to enter jigsaw mode (when all apps are rotating) and tap the icons at the bottom of the screen to see more.

Here you will see all the pages, there are signs at the bottom of the ground to show that they are strong.

Touching the page will turn it off, which means it won't change when you turn the pages normally. Once you have the option, tap it all, you're ready. If you notice that you have lost some pages, you can go to the accent tile and activate them.

How to use the library on iOS 14

In the Home Library, you'll see a folder on the grid that describes the type of application that contains each name. However, these are not standard discs, and Apple needs to do some divine work to do them. Each section has three main application areas and a cage in the lower right corner.

Ways to use the library on the latest iOS 14: Folders

The next touch will open the disk in a normal tile, but the app will open by clicking on something important (the apple that you know you're using all the time).

The only exception to this rule is that the help folder contains important features that you think will be useful on your iPhone right now.

How to use the library in iOS 14: Open folders

If you want to quickly find an app, but don't want to find folders, clicking on the scroll bar at the top of the page will open a list of all the apps it contains. Sequence You can change the search bar.

How do I get a library on my iPhone?

There are app libraries, new widgets, and an improved translator and comment system, as well as a map of all the features of iOS 14.

CHAPTER SIX

FAMILY SHARING

Use these methods to prepare family sharing. You can start a new family group and invite people to join or join someone else's family group.

Join the family group

Family sharing is easy for up to six family members to share App Store, Apple Store subscriptions, iCloud storage plans, and more without sharing the store ID. Set up Apple ID for kids, determine permission from screen time, agree to spend and withdraw from the parent device, and ask for a purchase. You can also set up Apple for your child or teenager or configure it with Apple Watch. Learn more about what you can do on the family side.

The family group should start

A family adult - a family manager - can arrange a family sharing for their iPhone, iPad, iPod Touch, or group of friends. If you change the distribution of sales, you will be asked to confirm that there is a payment method on your file as if you have agreed to pay for the sale initiated by the family you are calling. The best payment methods for setting up a family gift are credit cards and debit cards.

On your iPod iPhone, iPad, ,

Go to Settings> [Your Name].

Tap Share family, then click Set your family.

Follow the on-screen instructions to set up your family and ask your family members.

iMac

Select Apple System □> System Preferences list and click Family Share

You confirm the Family ID that you want to use for a family sharing and check the sharing from my purchase.

Follow the on-screen instructions.

Select Apple □ List> System Preferences and tap iCloud.

You confirm the Family ID that you want to use for a family sharing and check the sharing from my purchase.

Follow the on-screen instructions.

Invite people to join your family

If you haven't already done so, you can create an Apple ID for the child and add it to your group. If your family member has an Apple ID, use the steps below to add one to your family group. You can join one family at a time.

If you have a family member, he or she may enter your Apple ID password on your device to accept the request. You can also send them a request, and they can accept it from their device.

With your iPod iPhone, iPad,

Go to Settings> [Your Name]> Family Share.

Tap Add Member.

Enter the name of your family member or your email list and follow the on-screen instructions.

Choose whether you want to send invitations via messages or apply individually. Then follow the on-screen instructions.

iMac

Select Apple Pal ☐ List> System Preferences.

Click on Family.

Click Add Family Member and follow the on-screen instructions.

Select Apple ☐ List> System Preferences and tap iCloud.

Family Management.

Click the Family Member icon (+) and follow the on-screen instructions.

See if your family member agrees to the application

After you submit the invitation, you can check the status of the person under their name.

With your iPad, iPhone

Go to Settings> [Your Name]> Family Share.

The person's name has been chosen to see what the reception looks like. If you want to resubmit the invitation, choose to resubmit the call.

iMac

Select the Apple System □> System Preferences list and click Family Share. If you are using the OS Cause or are already using it, select Apple □ □> System Preferences> iCloud and click on Family Management.

The person's name will be chosen to see what the reception looks like. If you want to resubmit the invitation, choose to resubmit the call.

Join the family group

Accept or reject the application to access a family directly from your device. An application will be sent to you via email or comment. You can then respond directly by invitation. If you lose your email and text message, there is no problem. You can answer from your device settings or system preferences.

With your iPad, iPhone

Go to Settings> [Your Name]> Applicants.

To accept an invitation, follow the on-screen instructions. When you join a family, you will be sent

CHAPTER SEVEN

iPhone 12 CHARGER

During Apple's iPhone 12, the company boasted of its environmental initiative. Its data centers and stores are managed on a 100% renewable basis and the company aims to take it.

Apple's environmental innovation has surpassed corporate fees and malls. This year's iPhones don't come with earbuds, they're all names for healthy waste reduction. This will allow the iPhone to be delivered to the floor, and Apple will be the VP of the environment, policy, and social policy. According to Lisa Jackson,

Right now: Apple AirPods Studio displays malicious information

the environmental problems associated with the production, distribution, and distribution of resources will be reduced, it will also reduce pollution. Said by DRS

Still, there is a difference in Apple's new ecosystem. For all the good things the company does, there is always a secret design that stays and runs before its company's business operations. Apple is still connected to its official Lightning Protection port.

According to Apple, there are 2 billion iPhones subscribers in the world that, and they have not yet joined a third-party. Most of these chargers use a standard USB Type-A port. But it will be integrated into the iPhone 12 and will be USB Type-C with a lightning flash, so older players are not compatible.

At Apple stores this month, retailers can ask if they have a payment machine that has a USB Type-C connected. Some, not many. Yes, these users can also use their old 5W and Type-A plugs with power cables. But the new iPhone is fast-moving, and users can upgrade to the new high-end hardware. This prevents environmental benefits.

Nowadays, most of the tech world has turned to USB Type-C. All Android phones have been on the same standard for many years. Newer iPads and iPods also use the Type-C, so the standard of connectivity with Apple Plus is no different. The iPhone will be a support and will continue to work hard to connect iPhone users to old power poles as a means of keeping them in official port.

If Apple has switched to the Type-C, it could potentially provide the iPhone with a natural cable and adaptation ecosystem. Users with a new iPad can change their charging devices to catch the iPhone 12s. Android users jumping on the iPhone can still use the charging machines that come with their old phones. Or anyone who knows someone from his or her Android device will be able to restore their electrical settings.

Given the potential savings-potential benefits, Apple's decision to stick with electricity is quite different. Also, keep in mind that Apple is still keen to offer low-power small-C vessels worldwide to incorporate the new cable integrated into the iPhone 12.

It may come down to effectiveness. It's hard to say for sure why the power went out, especially since Apple has switched to USB-C on the iPad and the book, but one might say that the iPhone is the richest part of Apple, with the loss of electricity.

Although Apple has not disclosed manufacturing costs, it does mean that large-scale service is only two cents. So, even though production, boxing, and adaptation, and rope delivery come in dollars, with an impression of per share, it's easy money.

Currently, Apple is reporting sales of cables and chargers and other devices such as AirPods and Apple iPad.

CHAPTER EIGHT

SIRI

The official change of Siri for iOS 14 is its real invention. Instead of removing the entire screen, Siri now uses a smaller portion of your iPhone's display, allowing you to see the apps you're currently using.

While it has focused on network transformation, there are still a few things in Siri in the new announcement.

You can send audio messages on Siri with the iOS 14 update

Call Siri by pressing the button or by commanding "Siri".

Say "Send List ".

When prompted, enter the name of the contact the message was sent to.

After writing, stop talking or pause for a moment.

When the first message comes out, you will be asked if you want to submit it. Say "yes" as soon as possible.

Also, say "No", then click Cancel to leave the information blank.

You can view the information by clicking the button next to Capture in the compact box at the top of the screen.

What you see when you compose a video message with the Siri app in iOS 14

If you do not want to record a message, you can enter pre-written questions such as "Hey Siri, send an audio message to Felix".

How can the translation of Siri be improved?

Apple Play has introduced a new translation version of the original version, providing a minor series change over the years. It is ready for 2020 with little change.

First, Apple Play updated Neural Text to work outside of English text, including English text. This series will better understand all the translations and information.

CHAPTER NINE

SAFARI ON iPhone 12

This guide has the latest features and changes you will find in Safari for iPhone and iPad.

Generated version

OS 14 has a translation option in Safari, which translates the page into English, Spanish, Chinese, French, German, Russian, or Brazilian Portuguese, and has been added to update Apple's new translation program.

To access a website page in the Supported languages and translations section is as easy as clicking the "AA" button in the menu bar. Click Translate and the website page will automatically change the language on your phone.

Additional languages that you can translate can be added to the iPhone settings program.

Safari on OS 14 can track stored passwords by detecting data related to data breaches.

To illustrate this, Safari uses Safari duplication technology to verify your passwords, as opposed to a list of passwords that are considered secure and secure. If something crashes, you should notify Safari by giving us an idea to update your Apple login or generate a secure password automatically.

Websites that make money or use marketing networks for these purposes are just like any other website that uses analytics services like Google Analytics to collect information about website user behavior and project improvements.

Safari on iPhone and iPad, the number of browsers per website you visit, the number of blocked users, the number of websites you visit with the browser, and a list of common ways known as the Google Duplicate button.

The picture is in the picture

In Safari on the iPhone, if you see a video clip, you can browse another website to view it in window mode or click a button to do something on your iPhone. While the videotape is playing.

How to get started with websites

If you're typing a URL like Apple.com when you're downloading the search interface on an iPhone, you can click the "Go" button to open the website directly without typing. When linking to search results.

Easy integration with Apple Pal

Apple Play developers have created new tools for transferring website accounts to Apple, making it more convenient for iPhone, and iPad users who want to change the login with Apple.

Search permission

To provide personalized content, you need to obtain user consent for websites and applications you wish to search through websites. Enable the app to search or request not to have both options for the app, but the app is attached in a confidential statement so you can stay up to date on the app usage and website browsing habits.

CHAPTER TEN

HIDDEN iPHONE 12 FEATURES

The new Apple update for your iPhone 12 and iPad, home screens, business case, and many secret improvements. . After you set up your tablet, you can install iOS 14.

This update will enhance your experience, but my best strategies for iPhone 12 are what you need to do to get it. For example, you can now completely uninstall Apple Mail and Safari from Apple app settings.

Get it this way

Attach your email

I signed up!

By signing up, you agree to the CBS Terms of Use and the data system of our Privacy Policy. You can resign at any time.

Set your default email or website browsing

Apple will eventually let you manage your default applications. Currently, there is little documentation to do with email and website browsers. For example, Chrome may send a log to your browser or Outlook as an email of your choice.

App developers need to update their iOS 14 and a new default option will appear, so be patient if your app isn't ready for you.

To get started, open the iPhone or iPad app and scroll down to the list of all installed apps. Find the email or browser you want to click. If you've updated to iOS 14, you'll see the default app on the browser or Apple's default email; Click and select the application you like.

Quickly remove the home app screen

The new iOS 14 library, as an app downloader, allows you to remove some home screens that are not full of apps if you use them.

Hide the original screen panel

Do the following:

Tap the space on your home screen to get started in edit mode. Now, click on the page, click the checkmark below each banner you want to delete. This does not remove the applications but will take them to the computer library, where they can always access where the application is hidden or hidden in the box.

Customize-iOS-14

You can customize your iPhone's home screen.

Close the removed application on your home screen

If all your hard work is lost in the new project you just chose, you'll spend that time updating your home screen, adding widgets, storing your most important apps. Don't let them enter your iPhone on your home screen when you enter it, but send it directly to the Apple library until it's ready for it.

Open Settings> Home screen and just select the library above. You can find excerpts from previous libraries, just sit in the top right folder and look.

Check out the emoji keyboard

You can see an emoji area for your any emoji you will like to use. Launch the emoji keyboard as you like, and you'll find a scroll bar at the top of the keyboard.

Hidden image

Your hidden photo album can be hidden.

Hidden photos are now hidden

The ability to hide photos and videos or videos has long been available on iOS and iPad OS, but there's a big problem - you don't want to see these photos stored in an album. Hiding remote photo program

CHAPTER ELEVEN

iPhone CARPLAY

Upgrade CarPlay to iOS 14

iPhone 6s and later models will all update to iOS 14.

For CarPlay users, this new release will be even better, and we'll post all the details.

First of all, it has iPhone support, which can be used as a car kit. The new unit, used by BMW, previously allowed Apple iPhone owners to unlock and launch their cars with a push button.

Car key holding in lettuce will tell us how you pay through Apple Pal Pay. On iPhone 11, you can double-click the unlock button. Opening a car door is as easy as getting close to an iPhone, you have to put your smartphone in a locker or wireless charger when the machine starts.

The best is the full experience of the Watch Moment Clock running.

When you set a new car, users can lock it, start and run it, or stop the driver, so you can set boundaries. Motor vehicles can be distributed between transactions using messaging.

Another important thing to update this software update is support for Apple Wall and Wall documents. Starting with this update, users can browse sections and select the CarPlay Library UI in their headers. At this time, Apple does not allow users to rate their photos as wrappers, so they must first select a list of photos.

CarPlay is the latest update of iOS 14. With the release of this iOS, Car Play can run a number of applications, such as car rental or electric car rental. In addition, Apple allows the Food Order app to run on CarPlay, without any restrictions, optimized for the driving experience.

CHAPTER TWELVE

CHANGE APPS ICONS
iPhone 12

You can easily customize the look of your home screen by changing the auto-markers and photos you choose. Before following this guide, you should create an image of your software brand to download software online.

The exercises below explain how to add a custom logo to the home screen of a project that suits you.

Touch the application icon by entering the shortcut first, then touch the application

If you find it difficult to remove and manage shortcuts to the application whenever you open the application with custom looks or do not use the shortcuts you can use at all.

Shortcuts are a new tool, as they allow users to create different themes that work on their devices, but in this case, shortcuts have a common theme.

Launch shortcuts on your iPhone or iPad.

Choose that icon at the upper right corner side of the screen of your device.

Click Add-on.

Use the text field to view open applications.

Select Open App.

Select Select.

Use the browse command to change the icon and select it.

Type the three dots in the upper right corner of your device.

Reader application holder.

From the drop-down menu, select an image or select a file depending on the nature of the application.

Choose a shape to change.

In the text field, rename the section that needs to appear on the home screen.

Tap Add.

Tap Your shortcut is complete.

Return to the home screen.

If you already have apps on your home screen, you now have two features. To store your new logo, create an old icon in the library. You do not want to cancel the original request.

This process takes a long time, especially when you don't have to make all the requests when searching for or creating custom markers.

CHAPTER THIRTEEN

MAPS ON iPhone 12

With all the iOS updates, Apple will add new features to the instant operating systems, and iOS 14 is no exception. Most apps have new features, including a new moment map, including bike guides, EV tracks, guides, and more.

This guide outlines the new features and updates that Apple Play has added to the Maps app on the new iOS and iPad OS 14.

Bike guide

Maps on iOS 14 offer bike tips for first-time cyclists like Google Maps. Bikes, bike paths, and sidewalks tell you to go where you want to go.

You can check the height of your road, check the difficulty of the road, and see that the roads are congested. There are ways to avoid long cliffs or stairs to get your bike riding.

The Bike Guide and Watch are extended to Apple and Watch on OS 7, with easy navigation and voice guidance, as well as instructional maps.

The direction of the bike is limited to several major cities, including New York, Los Angeles, San Francisco, Beijing, and Shanghai.

Roads end with EV

If you have an iPhone-compatible electric car, it's important to add price tags to your system when planning your trip.

The choice of EV route is responsible for the time allotted for the arrangement of arrival times and for the use of maps that can verify the prices and types of sponsors to provide a planned route for vehicle owners. Electric vehicle

To use this feature you need to connect the electric car to the iPhone which does not work if you are planning to make a trip with your partner using the electric car because the space is not available if the EV is not available.

Currently, EM car parts and BMW and Ford vehicles are in operation.

Guidance

In iOS 13, Apple Play added "-direction-" "which allows you and your friends and family to create a timeline for visits.

You can still upgrade your devices to iOS / iPad DOS 14 ', but Apple is ready to take the lead in the trust.

Guide the best place to visit the city, as well as advice on places to eat, shop, and explore. Guides can be saved on maps and updated as new locations are added.

Other partners of Apple in the guide include Lonely Planet, Washington Post, Ultrails, Inspiration, and many more.

How to use the Apple Pal Map Guide

Apple Play last year unveiled a map with more details on roads, buildings, parks, beaches, oceans, forests, and more, with iOS 14 map spread across updated parts. Again.

Speed camera

If the machines and bright red cameras are running, Apple will tell you when they arrive. There is also an option to see where the camera is on the map.

Take advantage of the space

If you don't use GPS in the big city and the maps don't enroll you in the right place, a new update can be used to find the right place to read better.

Use your iPhone to scan nearby homes to minimize your time when choosing an iOS 13 app.

Because surrounding areas are used, cleaning is limited to areas including San Francisco, New York, Boston, Chicago, Houston, Las Vegas, Philadelphia, Washington, DC, and Hawaii. The cleanliness of the area was improved by the environment.

Integration

Decrease the incidence of easily accessible areas in big cities like Paris and London. IOS 14 maps show local prices and provide ways you can use them when you need them.

It's a city where licenses are restricted in some ways, and Apple Maps now supports license information, so you may decide you'll be allowed to use the route one day.